3/16

Taxes

What They Are and How They Work

ECONOMICS
in the 21st
CENTURY

Taxes

What They Are and How They Work

Lisa A. Crayton and Laura La Bella

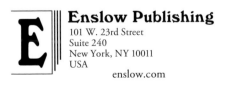

Enslow Publishing
101 W. 23rd Street
Suite 240
New York, NY 10011
USA
enslow.com

Published in 2016 by Enslow Publishing, LLC.
101 W. 23rd Street, Suite 240, New York, NY 10011

Library of Congress Cataloging-in-Publication Data

Crayton, Lisa A., author.
  Taxes : what they are and how they work / Lisa A. Crayton and Laura La Bella.
    pages cm. — (Economics in the 21st century)
  Includes bibliographical references and index.
  ISBN 978-0-7660-7376-0
  1. Taxation—United States—Juvenile literature. I. La Bella, Laura, author. II. Title.
  HJ2381.C69895 2016
  336.200973—dc23
                        2015029194

Printed in the United States of America

To Our Readers: We have done our best to make sure all website addresses in this book were active and appropriate when we went to press. However, the author and the publisher have no control over and assume no liability for the material available on those websites or on any websites they may link to. Any comments or suggestions can be sent by e-mail to customerservice@enslow.com.

Portions of this text were originally written by Laura La Bella.

Contents

When you plan out purchases, it's important to keep in mind how much sales tax you will also pay once you get to the cash register.

CHAPTER 1
Taxes Explained

H aving your own money to shop for clothing, shoes, CD, DVDs, video games, or other favorite "must-have" items is a dream come true for most students. One thing that quickly becomes clear, however, is that your money must stretch to pay for any taxes on your purchases. Rather than grabbing items that equal $100—the total you have for a shopping spree—you have to scale back depending on the amount of *sales* tax. That additional amount is added to the cost of your items at the register. You cannot opt out of paying the tax. It is mandatory, and everyone has to pay it.

If you have a job, you know firsthand about the mandatory tax all workers pay. That *income* tax represents the portion of income withheld to pay taxes. When you are offered a job, an employer promises to pay a certain dollar amount for every hour worked. Calculating your rate of pay is a simple matter of multiplying your total hours by the hourly rate. However, your paycheck actually will be less than that. The difference is the amount of *income* taxes deducted from your salary during that pay period. What a shock for many first-time workers!

If your hours and rate of pay remain constant each pay period, then your "take-home"—or net—salary will always be the same amount as that first paycheck. While it can be frustrating to see your hard-earned money go somewhere other than in your pocket, taxation is an important part of our government. Our Founding Fathers created a tax system in which each person in our country contributes money from his or her income to support our government. In turn, citizens receive needed services and enjoy ongoing protection, among other benefits.

Paying taxes is an important responsibility that comes with being a resident of a city, state, or country. What are taxes? Why are they needed? Who benefits from tax dollars paid? These and other questions are answered in this resource designed to help you better understand the role of taxes in our democratic society. The information in this book also will help you better understand your responsibility as a tax-paying citizen of the United States.

Taxes Defined

How can a few cents added to the purchase of a CD, Blu-ray movie, or other item you buy be that important? Learning about taxes and why we pay them is important to understanding how our government works.

In its simplest form, a government determines the way in which a country, state, county, town, city, or village is run. At every level of government, laws are created that citizens must obey. Policies are put in place for just about everything connected with our daily lives. A community—whether that community is a nation, a state, or the town where you live—needs an organized way to function, and a government provides that framework.

The US government provides public goods and services for the citizens of the country as a whole. But because our government doesn't generate an income of its own, it needs a way to pay its bills. The money that our government uses to pay these bills comes mostly from taxes.

Taxes have been a part of American history since our earliest days. In fact, taxation forced on the colonists by the British government was one of the

Some taxes are paid to the US government. This is a way
for it to pay for necessities like public schools.

reasons the colonists fought for independence in the first place. They drove
our nation's founders to declare war on Great Britain. However, when writ-
ing our Constitution, the Founding Fathers knew that our young country
would need the money generated from taxes to help build streets and roads,
buildings and parks, schools, and national defense.

Understanding Taxes

Simply put, our government charges its citizens taxes, which pay for services used by everyone. Taxes pay for services that citizens use in their daily
lives, such as the US Postal Service or police protection. They also pay for
services that protect our nation as a whole, such as the armed forces, which
protect the nation in times of war and peace.

There are two groups that collect taxes: the federal government and the state
government. The federal government taxes people by using a universal chart
based on a person's income. The chart is the same no matter which state you

Fire departments couldn't rush out to fight fires and keep
residents safe if it were not for state taxes.

live in. States work a little bit differently. Each state government can set the tax rate, or the amount of taxes people pay, and it can differ widely from state to state. Citizens pay state taxes in addition to the taxes they pay to the federal government. The reason for this is that each state offers services that are different from the services offered by the federal government. For example, federal taxes pay for the military when the United States goes to war, but state taxes pay for your local protection, like the city police force and fire department.

Common Taxes

There are a number of ways our government collects taxes. We pay different types of taxes depending on our income, the kind of purchases we make, and whether we own property or a home. The amount we pay in taxes varies as well. We may pay a higher tax on our income than we do for a clothing purchase at the mall. Among the most common types of taxes Americans pay are income taxes, Social Security taxes, sales taxes, property taxes, and excise taxes.

Income Tax

As its name suggests, income tax is tax that you pay on the money you earn from your job or investments, known as your income. Businesses also pay taxes on the money they make from selling goods and services. This type of income tax is called a corporate tax. Everyone who earns a paycheck pays a federal income tax, and forty-three of our fifty states charge their citizens a state income tax.

Federal income taxes support government programs, such as defense and education. The United States has what is called a progressive tax system. This means that the more money a person makes, the more he or she pays in income taxes. Someone who makes very little money pays a lower tax rate than someone who earns a very high income. Federal tax rates appear in a chart that assigns a tax rate to your income bracket. For example, if you earn between $0 and $8,350, you fall into the 10 percent tax bracket, which means you pay 10 percent of your income.

An income tax bracket is a category based on how much money you make. In 2014 and 2015, there were seven different tax brackets with these rates: 10, 15, 25, 28, 33, 35, and 39.6% percent. Also, your tax amount can be different based on whether you are single, married filing jointly (filing taxes together on one tax form), or married filing separately.

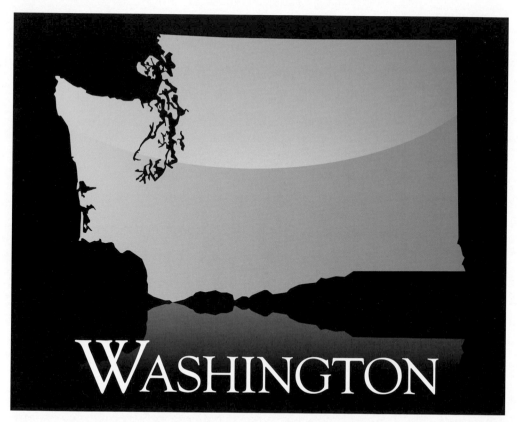

Washington is one of only seven states in the United States
that does not ask its residents to pay an income tax.

It can be hard to understand how your total taxes are calculated because you actually pay taxes at a given rate only for each dollar that falls within that bracket's range. For example, if you earn $9,350, the first $8,350 will be taxed at the 10 percent rate, but the last $1,000 will be taxed at the 15 percent rate. State income tax works in a similar way.

When you receive a paycheck, you may also pay state taxes on the money you've made. This is in addition to paying the federal income tax. There are only seven states that do not have a state income tax. They are: Alaska, Florida, Nevada, South Dakota, Texas, Washington, and Wyoming. State income taxes are usually much lower than the federal income tax rate.

Some towns and cities also impose local income taxes on their citizens. Again, this tax would be in addition to the federal and state income taxes you might pay. For example, in New York City there is a state income tax of up to 8.82 percent and a city income tax of up to 3.876 percent. These local income taxes help pay for local services, such as snow removal in the winter, public schools, and police and fire departments.

Social Security Tax

When you review your paycheck, you will see the amount of money you pay toward federal and state taxes listed on the pay stub. You might also see the word "FICA" next to a small amount of money that has also been withheld from your pay. This is the amount of money you pay in Social Security taxes. Also known as the Federal Insurance Contributions Act (FICA) tax, this tax helps fund Social Security. Social Security refers to a social insurance program that was created by the US government to protect its citizens against the effects of poverty, old age, disability, and unemployment.

Social Security, which is funded in part by taxes, is designed to help people when they can't work, such as in old age.

Sales Tax

Local governments impose a sales tax to raise money for local projects, like building schools and libraries, supporting prisons, and staffing fire and police departments. The rate varies from county to county and city to city. Sales tax is imposed on items you buy from stores, such as clothing, shoes, furniture, CDs, DVDs, and electronics. Automobiles are also taxed. Food purchases at restaurants are often taxable, but food purchased at a grocery store may be exempt.

Sales tax is called a flat tax, meaning that everyone pays the same amount of tax on an item. This tax is not based on your income. Even if you make more money, you will pay the same amount of tax on a sweater as someone who makes much less money than you do.

Property Tax

Property taxes are taxes that you pay on real estate. Taxes on land, and the buildings on it, are the biggest source of revenue for local governments. The village, town, city, or county where your property is located is in charge of collecting these taxes. Your local government decides the value of your real estate, such as your home, your business, or any other property you might own, and then determines how much money you should pay in property taxes. The money the local government raises is usually used for building schools, building and repairing roads and bridges, and snow removal. Property owners pay property taxes each year.

Excise Tax

Excise taxes, also called "sin taxes," are additional taxes people pay for items such as alcohol, tobacco, and gambling. These taxes are put in place to

Taxing Sugar

There's a new tax that makes a lot of people angry. The federal government is beginning to tax beverages that contain excessive amounts of sugar, such as soda, fruit drinks, and sports drinks. The people who work for companies that make these drinks are trying to prevent Congress from passing this new tax. Obesity is a growing health concern, especially among children. This tax would force people to pay extra to buy drinks containing sugar.

Cities are taking actions to try and impose their own taxes—not all have been successful. In 2014, Berkeley, California, became the first city to pass a tax on sugary drinks, including soda and sports drinks. The tax became effective in 2015 and imposes a one-cent tax per ounce of soda. San Francisco, however, voted no to a tax that would have added two cents per ounce on sugary drinks. In New York City, Former Mayor Michael Bloomberg could not get a tax imposed and his efforts to limit the sizes of soft drinks sold in restaurants also failed.

Those that support such taxes say that drinking sugar-sweetened drinks can lead to obesity, diabetes, and other health ailments. They say the tax would discourage people from buying these items and possibly reduce health problems. The soda industry says that taxes won't help teach children or adults how to make healthy choices. What do you think? Would a tax on these items change your buying habits?

Drinks that contain a lot of sugar, such as soda, are being taxed in some cities like California. Not everyone thinks this tax is a good idea.

help discourage the purchase of these items or, in the case of gambling, to dissuade certain behaviors. In the case of cigarettes, there is a federal tax of $1.01 added to the price of each pack. People also pay a state tax, which varies depending on where you live.

The top five states with the highest state tax on cigarettes are New York ($4.35), Rhode Island ($3.75), Massachusetts ($3.51), Connecticut ($3.40), and Hawaii ($3.20). New York City used to be the most expensive place to buy cigarettes in the United States. It is now the second most expensive, charging $5.85 in combined taxes—$1.50 city tax plus $4.35 state tax—per pack of cigarettes. Chicago is presently the most expensive place in the United States to buy cigarettes. There an additional $1.18 city tax is added to a Cook County tax of $3.00 and the state tax of $1.98. Combined, that's $6.16 in taxes (state, city, and county) alone that people pay when buying cigarettes in Chicago.

Excise taxes can affect the economy and influence consumer behavior. An excise tax is used to discourage the use of products and services that could pose a risk to someone's health, such as alcohol or tobacco. Luxury taxes are paid on expensive, nonessential items, such as luxury cars. Revenue from luxury taxes is redistributed through government programs that benefit all citizens. Do these taxes discourage the use of unhealthy products or the purchase of expensive items? Some consumers groups say yes, while others argue that no, they don't change behaviors.

Indirect Taxes

Taxes can be either direct or indirect. A direct tax is one that the taxpayer pays directly to the government. These taxes include income tax, Social Security tax, sales tax, property tax, and excise tax. These taxes cannot be shifted to others. An indirect tax is one that is passed on to another person or group. Fuel for our cars is an example of a tax passed on to consumers. The cost of fuel includes a tax that consumers pay, which raises the price of gasoline. Instead of oil companies paying that tax, they pass it on to consumers.

Collecting Taxes

When you pay taxes, the money goes to two places. The federal government and your state government both collect the taxes they charge on your income or on purchases you make at stores. The money the federal government collects is sent to the Internal Revenue Service (IRS). The IRS is a government agency that is responsible for collecting taxes. These taxes fund federal government services, such as the military and homeland security, Social Security, and health care services like Medicare and Medicaid. Taxes also support offices that have certain responsibilities, such as the Department of Education, which supports student achievement and educational excellence; the Department of Labor, which promotes the American worker; and the Department of Agriculture, which oversees food, food safety, and farming. Additional departments include the Department of Health and Human Services, which protects the health of the American people; the Department of Housing and Urban Development, which educates the public about home ownership; the Environmental Protection Agency (EPA), which helps maintain a healthy environment; and the National Aeronautics and Space Administration (NASA), which researches space and science, as well as many other offices and departments. Running the federal government itself costs money, too. Everyone from the president of the United States to the staffers that work in government agencies are employed by the US government. Their salaries and the costs of running each of these offices are also paid with the taxes collected from citizens.

Work done by the Environmental Protection Agency (EPA) to care for the environment, such as helping animals after an oil spill, is supported by taxes.

Most state governments that collect taxes send the money to a taxation department. This office is responsible for collecting taxes and distributing the money to state agencies to be spent on services for the public. State taxes help pay for public schools, police and safety, state-run colleges and universities, statewide roads and highway systems, and health and public services. These services include public assistance (also known as welfare), health programs such as Medicare and Medicaid, and other services that people use directly.

CHAPTER 2
The Need for Taxes

N o one ever claims to love paying taxes. At the same time, it is difficult to find anyone who does not benefit from taxes paid to city, state, and the federal government. Whether you walk or ride to school each day, for example, you experience the important role taxes play in communities across the country.

Sidewalks, streets, and bridges are built and maintained thanks to tax dollars. Cities use tax monies to build new schools or improve existing ones. Taxes fund school bus transportation programs that provide rides to students to and from school, and extracurricular activities. Salaries for crossing guards, teachers, and administrators all are paid from taxes. Finally, taxes also help schools pay for furniture, technology, books, and other important items used throughout the school day.

Your interaction with taxes does not end during the school day. Rather, monies collected from taxes also help pay for services you might use after school or on the weekend. Those include community pools and public libraries. And, if you—or someone you know—ever had to call 911 for a medical or fire emergency, you tapped into a vital community service provided by tax dollars.

Broad categories of services funded by tax monies, therefore, include federal services, such as Social Security, health care, national defense, and social services like food stamps. Our state income taxes and local taxes support services such as our public schools and libraries and maintenance on our streets, roads, and highways. They also support health care, prisons, and social services for citizens who have very low incomes or who need special assistance.

You, a Taxpayer

As a taxpayer, you are responsible for paying your taxes and filing a tax return. A tax return is a document that shows the federal and state governments what you are declaring as taxable. For example, taxable items on your income tax return include your salary, tips, and any income from a house or any property you own, such as rent paid to you. Everyone who earns a certain amount of income must file a federal tax return, which shows the federal government how much money you have paid in taxes. The federal government then reviews these forms and notifies you if you have paid too much in taxes or not enough. If you paid too much in taxes, you will get money returned to you. This is called a refund. If you have not paid enough, you will be told how much more you need to pay. Filing with states that impose an income tax works in a similar way.

In the United States, all tax forms are due to the federal and state governments by April 15 of each year. Because computers are now used to help calculate tax forms, you can file your forms electronically, which saves time and money. Our nation's tax system is a voluntary system. This means it is each taxpayer's responsibility to report all of his or her income. It is against the law to fail to report your income. It is called tax evasion.

Once you start working and earn a certain amount of money, you must start paying taxes. Some people work with an accountant for help filing their taxes.

Tax evasion is a serious crime. The IRS estimated that in 2007, Americans who didn't pay their taxes owed more than $345 billion in taxes. This is money that our government loses. People who do not pay their taxes can be sentenced to one year in prison for each year they avoid paying their taxes.

As a taxpayer, you have responsibilities. These include the following:

- Knowing when and where to file your tax return

- Keeping accurate and complete records of your income

- Giving the government (federal and state) accurate information on your tax returns

While taxpayers have a responsibility to file an accurate and timely tax return, they also have certain rights that protect them and the personal information they share with the federal and state governments. All taxpayers have the right to privacy of their tax information. Only authorized tax personnel can examine, or audit, a tax return. Even law enforcement agencies have no right to examine a person's tax returns. In addition, taxpayers have the right to appeal any IRS-proposed adjustments to a tax return or contest the results of an audit.

Sharing the Costs

As you have already read, each person pays taxes for services that are offered by federal, state, and local governments. Taxpayers often argue that they pay for services that they rarely use or will never use. We don't just pay for the services we actually use because very few people would have the ability to afford these services.

Think about it like this: If you had to call the police department to report that your car had been stolen, would you be able to afford the police services? What if you had to pay each time you drove your car on your own street? Someone has to maintain the roads, bridges, and streets that we drive on. What about the sewer and water systems in your town?

Would you be willing to pay each time you turned on your faucet for a drink of water? If we all had to pay each time we used simple services, we'd never be able to afford to live our everyday lives. With luck, you may never need to call your local police department, but if you ever do, isn't it good to know that you won't be charged a fee to report a crime or have an officer respond to your concerns? We pay for all of these services in the form of taxes so that they are available to society as a whole when needed.

How Taxes Are Calculated

When you understand why people pay taxes, you can see that each citizen is a vital part of society. Now is a great time to learn how all of these different taxes are calculated.

Federal income tax is based on a percentage of your personal income. The federal government uses a chart that everyone follows. The chart shows how much money a person makes and what percentage of income he or she will pay in taxes. The more money someone makes, the higher the tax he or she pays.

State taxes are calculated in a number of ways. For those states that have an income tax, the tax is based on a percentage of your income. Sales tax,

People pay taxes to fund the maintenance of utilities such as sewer and water systems. If we didn't pay taxes, we might have to pay every time we used them.

the tax paid when someone purchases items at a store, is a flat tax. That means everyone pays the same amount. For example, in New York City, most purchases are rung up with an additional 8.875 percent in state and city sales taxes. If you buy a CD for $10, the total cost of the CD will come to $10.89. The tax of eighty-nine cents is divided between the city and the state. The money is used for services offered to residents of New York City and New York State.

What is taxed as part of each state's sales tax varies by state. However, most states include the following: furniture, clothing, machinery and equipment, books, computers, boats, candy, cosmetics, cigarettes and tobacco, jewelry, art, collectibles, and building materials. There are some

Federal income taxes must be filed on or around April 15.
These taxes are based on a certain percentage of your income.

Receipts the E-Way

Technology is constantly changing how we shop. One of the recent innovations is the e-receipt, an electronic receipt for purchases. As usual, a cashier will ring up purchases. Depending on the store, either you or the cashier will enter the e-mail address where receipts are electronically sent. Once you pay, the e-receipt is immediately transmitted to the preferred e-mail address. The e-receipt usually arrives before the customer leaves the store. If you read your e-mail on a smartphone, you can pull up the receipt and review it within minutes of your purchase. You'll notice it looks very similar to a print receipt.

One benefit of this technology is the elimination of lost receipts. One disadvantage is that customers may not review these as carefully as a printed receipt. Take time to review your receipt. Check to make sure you receive any discounts. Also check to see how sales taxes were applied. This is especially important if you shopped at a big discount store that sells a variety of items like food, clothing, books, and music. In many cases, a "T" on the receipt means the items is taxable; "N" means it is nontaxable. If you find errors on your e-receipt return to the store as soon as possible—or before the store's return policy expires—to correct any discrepancies.

When you pay for a purchase on a mobile device, you get an e-receipt.
You can check for which items were taxed and see how much you paid.

Your First Job,
Your First Tax Filing

You won't have to deal with paying taxes until you start to work. When you do find employment—whether it's a summer job, a part-time job, or a full-time job—you will start paying taxes on the money you earn. Employees usually have taxes taken out of, or withheld from, each paycheck. When you start a new job, your employer will ask you to provide information on a form called a W-4. This form helps your employer determine how much money to withhold from your wages and how much to pay to the government on your behalf. It is important to fill out your form accurately and completely. It is also very important to keep accurate financial records. When you file your taxes, you should keep your records in a safe location for at least seven years. Remember, you can be audited, or have your returns and records reviewed by the IRS, up to three years after you file a return. Should you ever be audited, having your past financial records and a copy of your tax forms handy is crucial.

When you get your first job, taxes are probably taken out of your paycheck. You provide a W-4 form to your employer, which helps figure out how much to withhold.

items that are exempt from taxation in nearly all states. These exempt items include food, medicines and certain medical equipment, periodicals, and college textbooks.

Annually, the IRS conducts audits. A tax audit is an investigation into the tax documents filed by a person or corporation. Audits are used to ensure that tax documents are completed correctly and that all taxes that a person or corporation should be paying are actually submitted. A computer selects tax returns at random for auditing. Also, audits are done if the IRS detects unusual activity. On average, the IRS audits just one of every ninety-seven returns filed.

Taxpayers are also allowed exemptions and deductions. An exemption is an amount of money you can subtract from your income for being married and/or for having kids. Children are called dependents. Deductions are personal expenses that the government allows you to subtract from your income. These might include educational expenses, medical expenses, and business expenses, among others.

The Issue of Fairness

Some people pay more in taxes. Other people might use the services that taxes fund more than others. How do we keep taxes fair? There are two criteria used to measure fairness in taxes. The first is benefits received and the second is the ability to pay. Benefits received means that people should pay taxes in proportion to the benefits they receive in government goods and services. The ability to pay means that people's taxes should be in proportion to their resources.

Filing Choices

You can file your tax return in one of two ways. You can file electronically using a computer, or you can fill out the forms by hand and mail them in using the US Postal Service. There are key benefits to electronically preparing and filing your tax returns. These include increased accuracy, faster refunds, and the ability to file your federal and state returns simultaneously.

Tax filers can also fill out the forms themselves or hire a professional. Completing the forms yourself often requires the use of tax preparation software and a personal computer. The software gives taxpayers access to the latest rules and regulations. Also, using a computer enables taxpayers to transmit their returns from home, the workplace, or a library.

Hiring a professional means giving a tax professional your tax information. The tax expert then calculates the information on your behalf. Tax professionals can include certified public accountants (CPAs), tax attorneys, IRS-enrolled agents, or tax preparation businesses. Tax professionals charge a fee for preparing your taxes.

Many people leave the task of completing tax forms to professional tax advisers or accountants when it is time to file their annual tax returns. Choosing the right person for the job is important. You should look for someone who is knowledgeable about your state's tax policies and who will support you if the IRS decides to select your tax documents for audit. Think about what important questions you might ask a tax adviser to better understand why we pay taxes, where the money goes, and how to file your returns.

Today you can file taxes online, which is called filing electronically, from the comfort of your favorite chair. Some people still prefer to fill out forms by hand.

Ten Great Questions to Ask a Tax Adviser

1   Why do we pay taxes?

2   Why are there so many different types of taxes?

3   Where does our tax money go when it's collected?

4   What are my responsibilities as a taxpayer?

5   When do I file my tax return?

6   How do I file my tax return?

7   How are my taxes calculated?

8   What happens if I don't file a return?

9   What is a refund and how do I get one?

10 What happens if I am audited?

The American colonists expressed their opposition to the Tea Act by tossing tea into the river on December 16, 1773, now known as the Boston Tea Party.

CHAPTER 3
Historical View of Taxes

People and businesses complain about taxes as if taxation is a modern-day system. It is not. The practice started centuries ago, beginning with early systems used in Egypt and Rome. Back then, goods coming into and shipped out of countries were taxed. The custom of only taxing on imports and exports changed over time. Eventually, taxes were imposed on individuals for various reasons.

Our system of taxation is rooted in colonial life. It started with taxes used for regulating the economy. The focus switched when England needed money to pay for expenses related to fighting wars against France. It looked to the thirteen colonies for income. Its solution was a direct tax imposed under The Stamp Act. That early tax structure started in 1765 and required a tax on paper. The Stamp Act did not exclude paper based on usage. Rather, no paper was spared! Paper used for business and personal purposes was taxed. This included newspapers, legal documents, and even playing cards. Paper's role as a primary form of information exchange during that time makes it easy to understand how much paper—and tax collection—may have been involved. A change in focus from economy regulation to income generation troubled the colonists.

Our current system of taxation looks nothing like it did during colonial times. It has changed, evolving to meet the many financial needs of our country and citizens. There are federal, state, and local taxes. Our structure is flexible, allowing for increases and decreases in taxes as needed. One common increase occurs during war to pay for related expenses. A drop in taxes may happen during troubled economic times, like the recent recession, to give taxpayers relief and build our economy. One thing has remained over the centuries: taxes are unpopular and spark protests.

The most famous protest of taxation by the American colonies was the Boston Tea Party. On December 16, 1773, after officials in Boston, Massachusetts, refused to return three shiploads of taxed tea to Britain, a group of colonists boarded the ships and destroyed the tea by throwing it into Boston Harbor. The American colonists fought against the Tea Act for a number of reasons, but mainly because they believed it violated their right to be taxed only by their own elected representatives.

Declaring Independence

Even though colonists were forced to pay the tax the Stamp Act created, they were angry because they were financially supporting a government they had no say in running. This led to the rallying cry of the American Revolution: "Taxation without representation is tyranny."

As part of the American Revolution, in which America broke away from England and won independence, the country worked to create its own federal government. During this process, our Founding Fathers wrote the Declaration of Independence and the Articles of Confederation, which became the country's first constitution in 1781. A constitution provides a framework for the organization of a government. With the establishment

THE DECLARATION OF INDEPENDENCE.
JULY 4TH 1776.

Founding Fathers—here signing the Declaration of Independence—
included John Adams, Samuel Adams, Benjamin Franklin, Alexander
Hamilton, Patrick Henry, Thomas Jefferson, James Madison,
John Marshall, George Mason, and George Washington.

of this new nation, the citizens of the United States now had proper democratic representation. However, this new government made no money of its own and relied on donations from its states to provide it with an income.

The US Constitution replaced the Articles of Confederation in 1787. The document defined the three main branches of the government: the legislative branch, the executive branch, and the judicial branch. The legislative branch includes the House of Representatives and the Senate. Each state elected representatives to fill positions in the House and Senate, giving each state a voice in the federal government.

When the US Constitution was being written, our Founding Fathers knew that our country would need to raise money to build cities, establish roads, and create a military for protection. They also realized that the government could not function properly if it relied entirely on its states for its resources. As a result, the federal government was granted the authority to raise money and impose taxes on the American people. The Constitution gave Congress the power to "lay and collect taxes, duties, imposts, and excises, pay the debts and provide for the common defense and general welfare of the United States."

The Need for Funds

As our country has grown and evolved since it first declared independence in 1776, so have our taxes. Our government has made adjustments to the tax system as circumstances have created the need for more money. War and times of growth and prosperity have influenced taxation.

The United States first raised money from tariffs, which were the largest source of federal revenue from the 1790s to the beginning of the Civil War, when income taxes were established. A tariff is a tax, or duty, imposed on goods when they are moved from one country to another. The goods cannot continue on their way until the tax is paid. When the Civil War began, the US government needed more money to pay for the war. As a result, Congress passed the Revenue Act of 1861, which imposed a tax on personal income, or the money people made from working. This income tax was a new direction for our federal tax system, which until this time had been based mainly on excise taxes and tariffs. When it became clear that the Civil War would not end as quickly as the government thought it would, the federal government realized it would need more money. According to the website of the US Department of the Treasury, Congress created new excise taxes on such items as gunpowder, feathers, telegrams, iron, leather, pianos, yachts, billiard tables, drugs, patent medicines, and whiskey. Many legal documents were also taxed, and license fees were collected for many professions.

After the Civil War ended, the government realized it didn't need as much money, so the income tax was abolished in 1872. The Spanish-American War in 1898 created a renewed need for money, so taxes were established on items such as beer, tobacco, and gum. In 1913, the Sixteenth Amendment was approved. It allowed Congress to impose an income tax without dividing it among the states or basing it on the results of a census, which tracks the size of the population.

The United States' involvement in World War I greatly increased the need for revenue. Congress responded by passing the Revenue Act of 1916. The act doubled the lowest income tax rate from 1 percent to 2 percent and increased the top tax rate to 15 percent for those people who had incomes of more than $1.5 million. Our government was slowly realizing two problems: There was not an organized way to collect taxes, and not everyone paid their taxes. In 1918, only 5 percent of the population paid their income taxes, and yet it was this tax that was funding one-third of the cost of the war.

After the war came to an end, the economy boomed during the Roaring Twenties, a time in our country of social, artistic, and cultural growth. Increases in revenues from income taxes followed as people began to make more money. The United States saw a huge growth in industry as new technologies, especially cars and movies, grew in popularity. Taxes were cut five times to encourage the growth of the economy. But all of this came crashing down on October 29, 1929. Known as Black Tuesday, this was the day the stock market on Wall Street collapsed, plunging the country into economic despair. The event led to the Great Depression, when millions of people were out of work. People struggled to find jobs throughout much of the 1930s. As the economy shrank and people lost their jobs, there was less income to tax and the government felt the effects. Congress increased taxes to keep money coming into the government. The downside was that those who were lucky enough to have jobs saw a greater portion of their income go to the government. Also, many now believe that the tax increases further weakened the economy.

War's Economic Costs

When World War II broke out, the United States needed money to fund its involvement in the war. It was a very tense time for tax policy in our country. Everyone from the president to congressmen agreed that taxes needed to be high to create revenue to pay for the supplies our soldiers needed. In 1940, only around 10 percent of the population paid federal income tax. By 1944, just four years later, nearly every employed person paid income taxes. This tax money went toward soldiers' salaries, goods

During Word War II, only about 10 percent of people paid income taxes, but the government needed more money to fund the war. By 1944 the US government had expanded taxation so that nearly everyone who was employed paid taxes.

Taxation Without Representation Today

The citizens of the District of Columbia (Washington, DC) do not have representation in the US Senate. Washington, DC, is a district and is not recognized as a full-fledged state. As a result, a campaign has grown over the years for the district to have a senator or congressperson represent its interests. In November 2000, the DC Department of Motor Vehicles began issuing license plates with the slogan "Taxation Without Representation." In a show of support for the city, President Bill Clinton used the "Taxation Without Representation" plates on the presidential limousine.

When he was in office, President Bill Clinton's presidential limousine sported a "Taxation Without Representation" license plate.

they needed in combat, food to feed the troops, and equipment to support military efforts. World War II led to the creation of the Bureau of Internal Revenue, which later became the Internal Revenue Service (IRS). The IRS is the world's largest accounting and tax collection organization. The IRS created a "pay-as-you-go" system of tax withholding. In this system, taxes are withheld from each person's paycheck and sent to the government instead of individuals paying taxes in one lump sum each year.

While the pay-as-you-go system (which is still used today) made it easier for both the taxpayer and the tax collectors, it also reduced the taxpayer's knowledge of how much money is being collected. This made it easier for the government to raise taxes without taxpayers feeling the burden immediately.

Our government continued to make changes to our tax system as the country changed. In the 1980s, President Ronald Reagan drastically reduced taxes. His Economic Recovery Tax Act of 1981 reduced the amount of federal income tax for American workers. When many of the tax cuts the act created went into effect, the economy began a pattern of growth that lasted throughout much of the 1980s. The 1990s and 2000s saw a number of tax acts, from the Taxpayer Relief Act of 1997, which gave families a tax credit for each child in a family, to the Economic Growth and Tax Relief and Reconciliation Act of 2001, which cut taxes slightly.

Today, taxes continue to change and evolve as our government leaders look for ways to maintain or increase tax revenue while balancing the impact on the American worker. History has shown us that as our country enters wars and periods of economic growth and depression, and as the government needs more money to fund initiatives, taxes will continue to be raised and lowered to help support various projects.

When taxes go up, consumers need to factor in that extra cost when deciding what to buy. Even small increases on everyday items can add up quickly.

CHAPTER 4
How Taxes Work

While price is the most important factor affecting purchase decisions, the amount of taxes can quickly make an affordable item unaffordable. How high is too high? This question is one many consumers wrestle with every day when considering whether or not to buy products or services. For example, in supermarkets, retail outlets, and other stores a familiar scene plays out each day. Some people leave items at the register because they forget to calculate taxes when estimating the cost of those items. Shock, dismay, or disappointment sets in when the price is given. A decision is made about which items to keep or leave. This is one of the effects taxes can have on people and their decisions.

Changing With Times

Our federal and state governments can change taxes as often as they want to. All that's needed is for a new tax bill to be passed in Congress. Sometimes the government raises taxes to help pay for war or a struggling economy. Other times, taxes may be lowered to help taxpayers keep more money in their pockets. Taxes often change from year to year. Tax increases and tax cuts are both very common.

To understand the effect of a tax increase, we need to take a look at who bears the burden of the tax. For example, suppose the price of a T-shirt is $10 and the government imposes on shirt sellers a tax of 10 percent per T-shirt.

Taxing Matters for College-Bound Students

Taxes support education, especially public education. If you are college bound, you probably have heard a lot about the "Free Application for Federal Student Aid," or "FAFSA." Any student applying for scholarships, grants, or other financial assistance at any public or private college or university must complete the form. Did you know that tax information is vital to the accurate completion of the FAFSA? As a dependent child, you must provide and verify all income, including wages for you and your parents. Financial information is pulled from completed tax returns.

Here are some tips to speed up your FAFSA processing:

- Complete tax returns early. It is best to complete and file current returns after all W-2s and other financial documents are received from employers, mortgage companies, and other institutions. Keep in mind all returns will need to be filed with the IRS *before* filing the FAFSA.

- Complete by the FAFSA deadline date. This varies by state and selected schools.

- Link to the IRS. Schools require verified tax return information. When you complete the FAFSA you can link to the IRS data for all filed returns. As you complete the FAFSA it walks you through this process. This one step can eliminate the need to send or take a printed copy to your chosen school.

US First Lady Michelle Obama speaks at a workshop about how important it is for students applying to colleges to fill out FAFSA (Free Application for Federal Student Aid) forms.

A few weeks after the tax goes into effect, the tax causes the price of a T-shirt to increase to $11. The T-shirt sellers receive the same amount per T-shirt as they did before the tax, so the tax increase has not made the sellers worse off. Instead, consumers pay the entire tax in the form of higher prices. What if taxes are increased and instead of 10 percent per T-shirt the tax becomes 15 percent? That $10 T-shirt now costs $11.50. Would you buy it now that it costs more because of an increase in taxes? Now imagine how much more you would pay in taxes on items that cost thousands of dollars, like cars or boats.

A tax cut is a reduction in taxes. When a tax cut occurs, the government sees a decrease in the income it receives from taxes. Those who pay taxes see an increase in the amount of money they get to keep from their paycheck. Sometimes when taxpayers receive more money from a tax cut, they decide to spend it. This helps the economy grow. When people purchase more products, they pay more in local and state taxes, such as sales tax. But when the economy is bad and there is a tax cut, people tend to save any extra money they receive. This hurts the economy. While people have more money to spend, they are scared to spend it because they are unsure of what lies ahead. They think they might need that extra money in the future.

Allocating Tax Dollars

When the federal government collects our taxes, it uses them to pay for expenses that keep our government running. Each year the federal government creates a budget and makes it available for citizens to see. You might be wondering what our government spends our tax dollars on. Following is a sampling of programs:

> **Social Security/Medicare:** Retired people are eligible to collect Social Security once they reach a certain age. We each pay Social

Security taxes to ensure that one day we will receive this money back to help support us as we age.

Defense: This covers everything from military salaries to wars in foreign countries to the research, development, and purchase of new technologies.

Low-income programs: Some of our taxes go toward programs that help those who cannot support themselves. These programs include food stamps, housing support, and childcare assistance.

Interest on the federal debt: The federal government has debt and a lot of it. Taxes help us pay off the debt the government owes on loans.

Education: While states cover the majority of education costs, our government contributes to programs for low-income school districts, special education, and financial aid programs for college students.

When it comes time to go to college, remember that some tax dollars go toward funding the financial aid on which so many college students depend.

Health research: Keeping our nation healthy is important. Our taxes fund the Food and Drug Administration (FDA) and dozens of programs that keep our citizens healthy.

Veterans' benefits: The federal government provides income and health benefits to people who have fought in wars or worked for our military.

Community development: In the event of a major natural disaster—such as Hurricane Katrina, which destroyed much of the city of New Orleans, Louisiana—the Federal Emergency

After Hurricane Katrina charged through New Orleans, Louisiana, leaving devastation and destruction in her wake, taxes helped pay to rebuild communities.

Management Agency (FEMA) assists people in rebuilding their lives and communities.

Highways/mass transit: Most highway and mass-transit spending is supported by the taxes we pay. This includes roads, bridges, and bus and subway systems.

Prisons: Our taxes also support prisons and law enforcement programs.

Unemployment benefits: These programs temporarily provide benefits to people who are unable to find jobs.

International affairs: This includes the operation of American embassies abroad and contributions to organizations such as the United Nations.

Natural resources/environment: Taxes help fund national parks, federal lands, water projects, and environmental cleanup.

Agriculture: Farms may receive assistance from the government to be successful or to stay in operation.

The Federal Budget in America

The federal budget of the US government is created by the president of the United States and is sent to the US Congress at the beginning of the year, in January or February. Senators and Congress members make additional recommendations after they review the budget, and then the budget is sent back to the president for approval. Once the president approves the budget, it goes into effect on October 1 each year. Certain parts of the budget are mandatory expenses, such as Social Security and Medicare. But other spending is flexible. The government must decide what to fund and what

The US House Committee on the Budget, or the House Budget Committee, is in charge of overseeing the federal budget process, among other duties.

it may hold off on funding until the following year. Sometimes money is taken away from one area to support another. When the United States is at war, military spending increases, so cuts are made to other areas to help create a balanced budget and control overspending.

Are Taxes Necessary?

Getting rid of taxes altogether has been a proposed idea for some time. Although people would earn more money and their purchasing ability would increase, federal and state governments wouldn't earn any income from taxation and couldn't pay for services that are shared by everyone.

Without taxes, our country might not have the money to defend itself against war or provide even the most basic of services. The government would not be able to function if we did not support the people who run it. Local services used by those in need (e.g., public assistance, police, and firefighters) would need to be paid for by individuals, who could not afford them, and many services would simply disappear. There would be no maintenance on roads or bridges, and snow would not be removed in the winter months. If part of our country was struck by a natural disaster, no aid would be available to help the people in those communities rebuild.

Without taxes, where would the funds needed to repair public roads and bridges come from?

Working for the IRS

The Internal Revenue Service does more than just make sure you are paying your taxes. Because the IRS is a large federal agency, it has numerous career tracks to explore. While the IRS employs a number of accountants to check tax returns and answer questions when people need assistance in filing their tax documents, it also employs professionals with all sorts of professional backgrounds. The IRS hires lawyers, computer specialists, law enforcement agents, researchers and analysts, administrative people, and executives who participate in the highest level of decision making within the organization. To be hired by the IRS, you don't even need a background in math or accounting. The organization accepts applications from people with backgrounds in accounting, business, communications, information technology, computer science, law, research, and finance.

Tax Protests

Refusing to pay your taxes as a matter of conscience is called tax resistance. Tax resisters decide they no longer want to pay taxes because they disagree with how tax revenues are being spent or feel tax rates are unfair. Some protest the idea of taxes, and others even refuse to pay in an attempt to damage or overthrow a government. Refusing to pay your taxes is a risky thing to do and can result in penalties that include high fines and possibly time in jail or prison.

Tax evasion is when people use illegal means to avoid paying taxes they owe. Failing to file a tax return, failing to report all of one's income, or concealing income earned illegally (through gambling, theft, etc.) are all forms of tax evasion. Tax evasion is a serious crime and brings with it serious penalties. The IRS can fine a person for evading taxes. The fine includes the amount the person owes the government, plus a penalty amount that can total thousands of dollars. The IRS can also send you to prison for up to one year for every year you avoided filing your tax return.

Myths and Facts

Myth: You cannot be audited once you have received your refund.

Fact: Receiving your refund just means the IRS has reviewed your tax return and agreed with your calculations. That doesn't mean it won't go back to check that your filing is complete and accurate. Also, if the IRS receives a return from a separate party who names you and that information does not match your return, you can be audited. The IRS can audit a return up to three years after it is received.

Myth: Students are exempt from filing tax returns.

Fact: Many people believe that being a student means they don't have to file a tax return or pay their taxes. But it's untrue. Students must pay taxes on their income and file a tax return. Students do get special tax credits for being a student and can deduct some of their educational expenses, which may lower their tax bill.

Myth: My tax preparer or accountant is liable for mistakes on my tax forms.

Fact: The only person responsible for your tax documents is you, no matter who prepared them. Many taxpayers believe that if they use a professional accountant, that person is held responsible for any errors or omissions. Even if your accountant made a mistake, you will still need to pay for it.

CHAPTER 5
The Great Tax Debate

You've probably heard adults talk about taxes in unflattering terms. Perhaps they grumbled about the tax on common household items, a hike in income tax that reduced salaries, or the spike in gas caused by higher taxes. You may even have discovered a dislike for taxes after seeing your part-time wages reduced because of taxes.

Throughout history, people have criticized the tax system and questioned its effectiveness. Others have protested taxes and attempted to end taxation. No one has yet to suggest an alternative that would provide the same level of revenue taxes contribute to city, state, and federal budgets. The bottom line? Taxes exist because they fund valuable services at every level of government. The way we pay taxes might change in the future, but we will likely always pay taxes in some form.

As discussed earlier in this resource, one of the first demonstrations against taxation was the Boston Tea Party. On December 16, 1773, after officials in Boston refused to return three ships full of taxed tea to Britain, some frustrated colonists tossed the tea into Boston Harbor.

The colonists objected to the Tea Act because they believed they should be taxed only by representatives they elected themselves and not

Boston, Massachusetts, shown here in 2015, was the site of one of the first protests against unfair taxes, when people felt that the taxes on tea violated their rights.

by a distant government like the British Parliament. The event led to the Revolutionary War; however, it did not end taxation. The reality is that citizens need to pay taxes so that the government can function and provide for its people.

There have been other proposed tax plans that could replace the federal and state income taxes we pay. One such idea is the Fair Tax Plan, which would replace all federal income tax with a single, national retail sales tax. Instead of paying taxes on the money you earn from your job, you would pay a higher sales tax on all items you buy. Proponents of the plan say that there could be many positive outcomes from this new tax plan, among them the following:

- Federal income taxes would no longer exist.

- Financially challenged individuals would no longer be taxed, giving them more money.

- Current government services would continue to be supported because the money raised from a national sales tax would be equal to the amount of revenue earned from the federal income tax.

- People might feel that they have more control over how much they spend in taxes. Because the Fair Tax Plan is based on what consumers buy, people could exercise a certain amount of control over how much tax they pay by purchasing less.

- It would be much harder to avoid paying taxes. Because the current tax system is voluntary and relies on people to file their own tax returns, there are people who avoid paying taxes each year.

But with every new idea there are negative aspects as well. Opponents say that less-positive outcomes of the Fair Tax Plan could be:

- The price of goods and services would increase.

- If the income tax is not fully abolished, a future president and/or representatives could reinstate part of the federal income tax program in response to a national emergency or crisis. This could result in Americans paying both a higher national sales tax and a federal income tax.

- The plan could make it easier for the government to raise the tax rate on certain items that it deems unhealthy or dangerous, such as cigarettes, firearms, or junk food.

- The plan could cause an increase in crime. If the tax rate is too high, it could cause people to steal needed items and sell them for profit.

Tax Reform

Changing the way taxes work is called tax reform. Tax reformers, or the people who want to make the changes, are interested in changing the way taxes are collected and managed, reducing the amount of taxes people pay, and making the tax system easier to understand. Today, people try to reform or change the tax system by passing new laws. However, one of the first tax change efforts ever attempted was the Whiskey Rebellion of 1794, which turned violent.

The Whiskey Rebellion occurred when President George Washington decided to tax whiskey to help pay off the country's national debt. Farmers

US Tax System Facts

The US tax system is an amazing system that supports our nation and everyone living within its boundaries. When looking at the system's history, there are details that surprise most Americans, such as the fact that we started paying annual federal income taxes only in 1913. Back then, paying taxes wasn't as easy as having the money taken out of paychecks. Paying taxes annually required people to save money in anticipation of paying a lump sum to the federal government. It wasn't until World War II, when the government needed a steady stream of income to fund the war, that taxes were withheld from paychecks. This practice continues today. The American tax code has since become a complex system. Some say that it is the biggest, most complicated document ever assembled. Our tax code has more than seven million words and keeps increasing. Comparatively, the Bible only has about seven hundred thousand words.

thought the tax was unfair because they normally converted their excess grain into liquor as part of their livelihood. Also, it taxed the farmers for making whiskey, but not the people who bought it. Tensions grew out of control as farmers and other supporters protested and attacked tax collectors. Washington sent 12,950 troops to western Pennsylvania, near Pittsburgh, to put an end to the rebellion.

The Whiskey Rebellion is just one of the many events in history in which the American people have tried to reform the tax system. As new ideas have been introduced, some guiding principles on how to judge tax reform proposals have been developed. First, new tax systems should be simple so that taxpayers can understand the amount of taxes they are paying. Also, they should clearly instruct people on how to pay their taxes and offer deadlines and easy ways to make payments. New tax systems should be fair to the poor, the middle class, and the wealthy. Finally, it should be clear to people what is being taxed (income, property, purchases) and at what rate or percentage. The truth is, even though there will always be new proposals for how to collect taxes, we need to pay taxes to help our government operate efficiently.

When farmers, but not consumers, were forced to pay taxes for making whiskey, farmers' supporters in Pennsylvania protested violently. This became known as the Whiskey Rebellion.

Living Without Taxation

What would our country be like if we paid no taxes? Can we live in a tax-free society? There have been organizations and groups that have suggested that we end the current taxation system and adopt a tax-free society. These groups have suggested many ways to create this system. One proposal is for every person to donate a certain amount of money to a trust fund. A trust fund is an account to which money is added and the interest is paid to the party named on the trust. In this case, the American people would donate money to a trust, and the government would receive money from the trust to support the operation of the government.

Suppose we lived in a society without taxation. If there were no taxes, the government would not earn any income from taxation and citizens would not spend their hard-earned money on taxes. If someone had a wage of $10 an hour, he or she would be able to keep the entire amount. Many people in support of a society without taxation think that if taxation did not exist, people would spend more money. Maybe they would even work harder, knowing that they could keep every cent they earned.

What about the opposite situation? What if taxes were 100 percent of your income? In other words, every cent of what you earned would go to the government. If you didn't get to keep any of the money you earned, would you work? Most likely, you would not. What would be the point?

There are a few countries that have tax-free societies. The Cayman Islands, located in the Caribbean Sea, do not impose income or property taxes. The country's government raises money through taxes placed on importing and exporting goods and on fees charged to tourists, work permit fees, and transaction fees. This may be an extreme example, but it shows us how society could operate in such a scenario.

Bermuda is one of just a few societies in which the government does not impose taxes on its people.

Pay Up!

Imagine being a millionaire pop star or athlete. Do you think it would be easier to pay taxes because you have lots of money? The reality is that each year numerous famous people, including pop stars and athletes, don't pay taxes. Tax evasion is a crime! When it is discovered, there are stiff penalties to pay. Some people are able to pay back taxes and avoid prison. Others are sent to prison. Penalties, including possible imprisonment, vary based on the amount of monies owed the government and how long taxes remained unpaid. Paying taxes is not optional. Whether you work for someone else or start your own business, develop a good habit of tracking your income and paying your taxes timely!

Ty Warner, founder of the company that made Beanie Babies, was tried and convicted for tax evasion. He did not go to jail, but he paid millions in penalties.

Freedom to Pay Taxes

As American citizens, we all share the same freedoms. Because we all partake of the benefits that this affords us, we should contribute to making our country the best place to live. Taxes give us that opportunity.

While there are many different systems of taxation in the world, every one of them has its pros and cons. It may not be a perfect system, but the US government has stuck to this current tax system because it works.

CHAPTER 6
Taxes and the Digital Revolution

aper ruled our taxation system in its early years. Your grandparents may remember receiving their IRS 1040 Forms in the mail. Libraries, post offices, and other public venues also had blank copies available for pickup. Taxpayers mailed returns backed to the IRS. Processing of returns took weeks and tax refunds were mailed to recipients' preferred addresses.

E-Filing

The digital revolution has changed much of that. In the 1980s, tax preparers began using computers for electronic tax preparation. The IRS did not have a system in place for receiving electronic tax forms. Tax preparers, therefore, printed them out for their clients for signature and mailing to the IRS.

That changed in 1986 when the IRS launched an e-filing pilot program. It initially accepted only returns for individual taxpayers receiving refunds. Five tax preparers volunteered to participate and were responsible for filing twenty-five thousand returns. While an improvement over the traditional way of filing and receiving tax returns, that initial process required manual use of special equipment and telephone calls to preparers regarding acknowledgments. Changes were needed.

Since 1986, the IRS has offered the option to e-file. Although it had a rough start, the bugs were worked out and today e-filing is mandatory in some cases.

Over time, the IRS made further improvements to its system. Taxpayers also became increasingly comfortable with the new technology and started using it more. The IRS reports that 2011 was a record year for electronic returns with more than one hundred million returns filed!

What a difference technology made in just twenty-five years. Filing electronic returns is optional. If you want to file a paper return you may do so. Benefits of using the technology, however, include the following:

- **Less hassle.** Tax returns have to be postmarked by the IRS deadline, April 15 (unless it falls on a Saturday or Sunday). Many people wait until the deadline to file. Returns need a postmark

By taking advantage of e-filing on the IRS website (www.irs.gov), users can often get their returns back and into their bank accounts much faster.

Over the years, the IRS has constantly refined its system,
such as improving organization and upgrading its computer systems.

showing it was mailed by the deadline, resulting in long lines at post offices. E-filing avoids that hassle.

- **Quicker status updates.** Generally, in about two weeks or less the IRS website provides a status update when a return has been received. Later, the update shows expected release date of any refund. This eliminates the need to call the IRS, a lengthy process with long wait times during tax season.

- **Faster processing of refunds.** The IRS estimates longer times to process returns mailed to its offices.

Taxing Matters

As you work and earn more, you may need increased documentation to file taxes. The digital age, however, has evolved to make it easier for you to receive information. Large pharmacy chains offer electronic statements of prescriptions and eligible medical supplies for providing that information on returns, if needed. Banks offer electronic mortgage statements. Credit card companies provide electronic statements listing annual expenses for use in deducting eligible business expenses. Colleges and universities also provide electronic copies of tuition statements.

Tax preparation companies like H&R block offer online e-filing using their software and e-funds. Technology has also spurned new companies that exist to offer loans against anticipated refunds. Many of these offer immediate access to those funds. Before using any of these companies, know that most charge a fee. Be careful how you share your financial information online, and ask advice from a parent or financial advisor before using an

Pay Outstanding Taxes

With each paycheck you will pay taxes on your salary. At the end of the year, you might still owe additional taxes if you do not have enough deductions taken from your paychecks. It is best to pay those as soon as possible. Get help from a parent or financial professional if needed, assuring your payment is properly identified and submitted to the IRS. What options are available?

- Submit a check. Include a check with your paper filing.

- Pay by phone. Call the IRS to make a payment.

- Authorize a debit from your bank account. You can pay directly from your bank account at the time you e-file.

- Pay online. Use a debit or credit card to make a payment.

- Make a payment arrangement. The IRS may allow you to pay your outstanding taxes over time rather than in one lump sum payment.

For any of these options, check the IRS's website at www.irs .gov for any special instructions. Keep a record of your payment with a copy of the related tax return. You may need the receipt in the future.

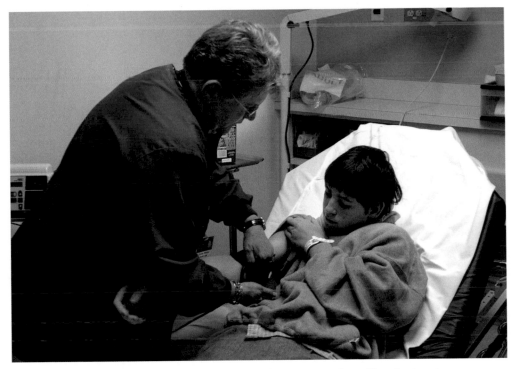

If you need a prescription, many drug companies offer electronic statements for those prescriptions and eligible medical supplies in case you need this information for your tax return.

Internet-based only company or one that has only been in existence for a couple years.

Your Tax Dollars Matter

The US taxation system is complicated, yet effective. It continues to work because taxpayers take their responsibilities seriously—even while complaining about the structure. President James Madison once said, "The power of taxing people and their property is essential to the very existence of government." This remains true today. *Your* tax dollars help to make our democratic society meet the needs of all citizens, including yourself.

Timeline of Taxes

December 16, 1773 Boston Tea Party. Colonists revolt against increased tax on tea and other imports.

July 4, 1776 Continental Congress adopts Declaration of Independence.

December 15, 1777 The Continental Congress passes the Articles of Confederation.

March 1, 1781 Articles of Confederation ratified by all thirteen states.

1787 US Constitution replaces Articles of Confederation.

1794 Whiskey Rebellion sparked by rebellion to tax on whiskey.

1861 Congress passes Revenue Act of 1861, establishing first annual income tax, to pay for Civil War expenses.

1872 Income tax abolished.

1898 Taxes imposed on beer, tobacco, gum, and other items to raise monies needed for Spanish-American War.

1913 Sixteenth Amendment approved allowing Congress to impose income tax. The first "Form 1040" was introduced for reporting income.

1916 World War I increases need for revenue. Congress passes Revenue Act of 1916.

1920s Income tax revenue increases during "Roaring Twenties."

1929   Stock Market Crash leads to increased taxes in the 1930s.

1944   Creation of Bureau of Internal Revenue.

1950s   Bureau of Internal Revenue name changed to Internal Revenue Service.

1976   Former President Gerald Ford becomes first president to publicly release personal income tax.

1986   The IRS launches an e-filing pilot program.

January 1, 2012   IRS requires most tax return preparers to file taxes electronically.

Bibliographic Sources

American Institute of Certified Public Accountants. "Understanding Tax Reform: A Guide to 21st Century Alternatives." AICPA.org, October 17, 2005. Retrieved August 11, 2009 (http://tax.aicpa.org/ Resources/Tax+Advocacy+for+Members/Tax+ Legislation+and+Policy/ Understanding+Tax+Reform+A+Guide+to+21st+Century+Alternatives .htm).

Anthony, Joseph. "7 Tips for Hiring a Tax Pro." Retrieved August 12, 2009 (http://businessonmain.msn.com/knowledgeexchange/articles/ adaptingandgrow.aspx?cp-documentid=18964878).

Boonn, Ann. "State Cigarette Excise Tax Rates & Rankings." Campaign for Tobacco-Free Kids. June 30, 2015. Retrieved July 7, 2015 (https:// www.tobaccofreekids.org/research/factsheets/pdf/0097.pdf)

Boonn, Ann. "Top Combined State-Local Cigarette Tax Rates (State plus County plus City)." Campaign for Tobacco-Free Kids. Retrieved July 7, 2015 (https://www.tobaccofreekids.org/research/factsheets/ pdf/0267).

Boortz, Neal, and John Linder. "The Fair Tax Book: Saying Goodbye to the Income Tax and the IRS." New York, NY: Harper Paperbacks, 2006.

Cayman.com. "Benefits of Living in a Tax Free Country." October 9,
    2008. Retrieved August 8, 2009 (http://cayman.com.ky/about-
    cayman/financial-services/benefits-living-in-tax-free-country.html).

Colonial Williamsburg. "A Summary of the 1765 Stamp Act." History
    .org. Retrieved August 11, 2009 (http://www.history.org/history/
    teaching/tchcrsta.cfm).

Detweiler, Gerri. "Does Your Teen Really Have to File Taxes?" *USA
    TODAY.* March 28, 2015. Retrieved July 6, 2015 (http://www
    .usatoday.com/story/money/personalfinance/2015/03/28/credit-
    dotcom-teen-taxes/70492044).

Dugdale, Emily. "Soda Tax Raises $116,000 of Revenue in First Month,"
    May 18, 2015. Retrieved July 6, 2015 (http://www.berkeleyside.com/
    2015/05/18/berkeley-soda-tax-raises-116000-revenue-in-first-month/).

Hoffman, Rosalyn. *Smart Mama, Smart Money: Raising Happy, Healthy
    Kids Without Breaking the Bank.* New York, NY: New American
    Library, 2012.

Huddleston, Cameron. "Five Steps to Hiring a Tax Pro." January 2009.
    Retrieved August 9, 2009 (http://www.kiplinger.com/features/
    archives/2007/02/taxpro.html?kipad_id=49_).

Internal Revenue Service. "Brief History of IRS." Retrieved July 6, 2015
    (http://www.irs.gov/uac/Brief-History-of-IRS).

Internal Revenue Service. "Internal Revenue Bulletin: 2014-47."
    November 17, 2014. Retrieved July 6, 2015 (http://www.irs.gov/
    irb/2014-47_IRB/ar14.html).

Internal Revenue Service. "IRS E-File: A History." Retrieved July 6, 2015 (http://www.irs.gov/uac/IRS-E-File:-A-History).

Internal Revenue Service. "Understanding Taxes." IRS.gov. Retrieved August 10, 2009 (http://www.irs.gov/app/understandingTaxes/student/index.jsp).

Intuit Turbotax. "A Brief History of Income Taxes." Retrieved July 6, 2015 (http://images.turbotax.intuit.com/iqcms/marketing/lib/fun/historyoftaxes/history-of-US-taxes-infographic-800.jpg).

Karlonia blog. "Fair Tax Pros and Cons." Karlonia.com, April 16, 2007. Retrieved August 11, 2009 (http://www. karlonia.com/2007/04/16/fair-tax-pros-and-cons).

Kaufman, Wendy. "Random Tax Audits Return to the IRS." October 9, 2007. Retrieved August 11, 2009 (http://www.npr.org/templates/story/story.php?storyId=15111003).

McCormally, Kevin. "Don't Worry About an Audit." March 21, 2008. Retrieved August 14, 2009 (http://www.kiplinger.com/columns/taxtips/archive/2006/tax0216.html).

Mian, Atif, and Amir Sufi. *House of Debt: How They (And You) Caused the Great Recession and How We Can Prevent It From Happening Again.* Chicago, IL: The University of Chicago Press, 2014.

New York State Department of Taxation and Finance. "2014 Tax Tables." Retrieved July 7, 2015 (http://www.tax.ny.gov/pit/file/tax_tables.htm).

New York State Department of Taxation and Finance. "New York City Tax Rate Schedule." Retrieved July 7, 2015 (www.tax.ny.gov/pdf/current.../it/nyc_tax_rate_schedule.pdf).

Parrish, Geov. "Why Pay Taxes?" April 3, 2006. Retrieved August 11, 2009 (http://www.commondreams.org/views06/0403-27.htm).

PBS. "How Does Government Affect Me?" PBS.org. Retrieved August 12, 2009 (http://pbskids.org/democracy/govandme).

Retirement Living Information Center. "Taxes by State." Retirement Living.com. Retrieved August 10, 2009 (http://www.retirement living.com/RLtaxes.html).

Saching.com. "Importance of Taxes: Why Should We Pay Tax to the Government?" June 18, 2009. Retrieved August 11, 2009 (http://www.saching.com/Article/Importance-of-taxes--Why-should-we-pay-tax-to-the-government/2682).

Saunders, Laura. "High Earners Facing First Major Tax Increase in Years." *The Wall Street Journal*, January 1, 2013. Retrieved July 6, 2015 (http://www.wsj.com/articles/SB1000142412788732382010457821609204302 2764).

Schnepper, Jeff. "5 Tax Myths That Can Cost You Money." July 6, 2009. Retrieved August 8, 2009 (http://articles.moneycentral.msn.com/Taxes/AvoidAnAudit/5taxMythsThatCanCostYouMoney.aspx).

Schoen, John W. "How the Government Spends Your Taxes." MSNBC.com, April 3, 2008. Retrieved August 2, 2009 (http://www.msnbc.msn.com/id/23924282).

Tax History Museum. "An Overview of US Taxation History." Retrieved July 2, 2015 (http://www.taxhistory.org/www/website.nsf/Web/TaxHistoryMuseum?OpenDocument).

Tax World. "A History of Taxation." Taxworld.org. Retrieved August 12, 2009 (http://www.taxworld.org/History/TaxHistory.htm).

TeenAnalyst. "Introduction to Taxes." TeenAnalyst.com. Retrieved August 13, 2009 (http://www.teenanalyst.com/taxes/introtaxes.html).

TeenAnalyst. "Types of Taxes." TeenAnalyst.com. Retrieved August 10, 2009 (http://www.teenanalyst.com/taxes/varioustaxes.html).

Thompson, Derek. "How Teenagers Spend Money." *The Atlantic.* April 12, 2013. Retrieved June 5, 2015 (http://www.theatlantic.com/business/archive/2013/04/how-teenagers-spend-money/274949).

US Department of the Treasury. "History of the US Tax System." Retrieved August 11, 2009 (http://www.treas.gov/education/fact-sheets/taxes/ustax.shtml).

Glossary

audit—A review of your tax return by the IRS, during which you may be asked to prove that you have correctly reported your income, deductions, and exemptions.

debt—Something that is owed, such as money, goods, or services.

deduction—An expense you are permitted to subtract from your taxable income before figuring your tax bill.

dependent—Someone you support and for whom you can claim a dependency exemption on your tax return.

direct tax—A tax that is paid directly to the government, such as income tax.

electronic filing—Filing your tax documents online. It is the fastest way to get your tax return to the IRS (and your state's revenue office).

excise tax—A tax that is imposed on certain goods to discourage people from buying them.

exemption—An amount of income exempted from taxation. Taxpayers can claim a personal exemption for themselves and for a spouse. Taxpayers can also claim an exemption for a child or other dependent.

federal taxes—Taxes that are paid to the federal government.

FICA—The Federal Insurance Contributions Act tax, which pays for Social Security and Medicare.

flat tax—A term used to describe a tax rate that always stays the same.

import tax—A tax imposed on goods when they are moved across a political boundary.

income—The amount of money you earn.

income tax—A tax on the total amount of money you make in a given year.

indirect tax—A tax that is paid to an intermediary, who then pays the tax to the government. Sales tax is an example of an indirect tax.

net salary—The amount of money you earn each year after taxes are paid.

parliament—The legislative body of Great Britain, which has the power to pass and amend laws.

progressive tax—A tax in which the tax rate increases as the taxable amount increases.

property tax—A tax on the value of any real estate you own, such as land or buildings.

rebellion—An organized refusal to obey certain laws.

revenue—The income of a government from taxes and other sources.

sales tax—A tax charged at the point of purchase for certain goods and services.

state taxes—Taxes that are paid to the state government.

tax bracket—A division by which the amount of income taxes you pay is defined.

tax credit—A tax incentive awarded to qualifying taxpayers, such as students. The amount of the credit is subtracted from the taxes you owe the government each year that you qualify.

tax evasion—Avoiding taxes intentionally and by using illegal tactics.

tax reform—The process of changing the way taxes are organized, collected, and managed by the government.

tax resistance—Refusing to pay your taxes because you do not agree with government policies.

tax return—A document filed by a taxpayer that gives the government an outline of what he or she owes in taxes for a given year.

veteran—A person who has served in the armed forces.

withholding—The amount held back from your paycheck that is used to pay your income and Social Security taxes.

Further Reading

Books

Conaghan, Daniel. *The Book of Money: Everything You Need to Know About How Finances Work*. Buffalo, NY: Firefly Books, 2013.

Gagne, Tammy. *Teen Guide to Earning Income* (Practical Economics for Teens). Hockessin, DE: Mitchell Lane Publishers, 2014.

Gamm, Scott. *More Money, Please: The Financial Secrets You Never Learned In School*. New York, NY: Plume, 2013.

Kiyosaki, Robert T. *Rich Dad Poor Dad for Teens: The Secrets about Money—That You Don't Learn in School*. 2nd Edition. New York, NY: Plata Publishing, 2012.

McGuire, Kara. *All About the Green: The Teens' Guide to Finding Work and Making Money*. North Mankato, Minn.: Compass Point Books, 2015.

McGuire, Kara. *Making Money Work: The Teens' Guide to Saving, Investing, and Building Wealth* (Financial Literacy for Teens). Mankato, MN: Compass Point Books, 2015.

Nichols, Clive. *Taxes and Government Spending* (Dollars and Sense: A Guide to Financial Literacy). New York, NY: Rosen Publishing Group, 2012.

Sylvester, Kevin. *Follow Your Money: Who Gets It, Who Spends It, Where Does It Go?* Toronto, Canada: Annick Press, 2013.

Tyson, Eric. *Personal Finance For Dummies.* Hoboken, NJ: John Wiley & Sons, Inc. 2012.

Watkins, Heidi. Book Editor. *Consumer Culture. Issues That Concern You.* New York, NY: Greenhaven Press, 2011.

Websites

Certified Public Accountant Carol Topp's Website
microbusinessforteens.com
Articles, blog posts, podcasts, and e-books on money topics for teens.

Junior Achievement's $ave, USA Interactive Lessons
www.juniorachievement.org/web/ja-usa/courseware
Interactive lessons on money management.

***Start Here* Magazine**
www.startheregoplaces.com/why-accounting/start-here-magazine/
American Institute of Certified Public Accountant's magazine regarding accounting careers and other related information for students.

Tax History Museum
www.taxhistory.org/www/website.nsf/Web/TaxHistoryMuseum?Open Document
An overview of US taxation history.

The Mint
www.themint.org/teens
Resources on various money topics provided by Northwestern Mutual.

Tic Tac Taxes Game

www.econedlink.org/interactives/EconEdLink-interactive-tool-player.php? filename=em370_TicTacTaxes.swf&lid=370

Tax-related game based on "tic-tac-toe."

Index